52 Thoughts
about
Thoughts

Reflections & Considerations
for Life's Journey

Audrey Alexander

52 Thoughts About Thoughts
Reflections & Considerations for Life's Journey

Copyright © 2022 by Audrey Alexander

RHG Media Productions
25495 Southwick Drive #103
Hayward, CA 94544.

ISBN 979-8-218-02074-3

Visit us on line at www.YourPurposeDrivenPractice.com
Printed in the United States of America.

Dedicated to

My ancestors and descendants

and

Sophia Ruach von Deus

With Gratitude to…

Judi

Matt

Jennifer

Ellen

Paul

Ed

Terry

Charles

Rebecca (my umbilical cord to reality), Natasha, Misti, Suanne, Shannon, Simona, and all at Your Purpose Driven Practice and RHG Media Productions.

CONTENTS

INTRODUCTION

The purpose of this book is to invite thought and conversation. This book makes no attempt to delve deeply into any particular subject.

The reader is presented with a quote and my thoughts on the quote. If you agree with my thoughts, great! But take it a step further and think about *why* you agree. If you disagree with my thoughts, OK, too! But take it a step further and think about *why* you disagree.

Teens through PhDs can explore topics to think about and discuss. Maybe new insights will inspire the reader to learn more about a particular topic. Maybe one of the reflections will offer a perspective not heretofore imagined and evoke mindfulness of multiple depths of understanding.

If any of the reflections brings a smile; if any of the reflections inspires the reader to say, "I've never thought about it like that before;" if any of the reflections helps someone to reframe a personal situation, then this book will have served its purpose.

Enjoy the journey, my friend.

Namaste.

Gratitude Begets Joy

"Gratitude is not only the greatest of
virtues but the parent of all others"[1]
—Cicero

On my grandson's sixth birthday, we were in the midst of the pandemic. Because of isolation restrictions, instead of a party, his parents hosted a drive-by birthday parade in front of his home. More than a dozen cars gathered in a strip mall parking lot at the end of the block where he lives, and at the appointed time, we were to drive down the street, honk horns, and wave at him. Some folks decorated their cars with streamers; some had happy birthday signs taped to their car doors. I made a poster with pictures of animals cut out from magazines and held it out the sky roof in my car when I passed him.

While we were waiting in our cars for the drive-by parade to begin, a police car pulled into the lot we were parked in. I didn't know what was going on, so I cracked open the driver's side door, slunk out, crouch-walked until I got behind my car, then slithered over to the next car and said *PSSST* to the person standing in front of that car. I whispered, "Why are the police here? Are we in trouble?" She said, "The police are going to escort us and lead off with sirens to start the parade."

Oh. I walked normally back to my car. Turns out the police being there was a good thing. I was prepared to jump into my car and peel away if we were in trouble with the law (like I could outrun the police in my very old V-4 engine Toyota).

Anyway, a little after 6 PM, the police turned on their sirens, and we followed them down the block honking and waving and shouting HAPPY BIRTHDAY! Each car had less than 15 seconds to wish him a happy birthday because "the parade must go on!" Through the sunroof I handed his dad my homemade poster and shouted, "I love you, Buddy Friend!" He said, "Love you, too, Grammy." And then I drove away.

On the way home, I just started sobbing. Can't even tell you why. Just sobbing and sobbing some sort of sad-happy tears.

I was sad because:

1. I couldn't hug my grandson on his birthday.

2. I had 15 *seconds* with him.

3. How sad the "new normal" was on a child's birthday.

I was happy because:

1. I got to see my beloved grandson on his birthday! Some grandparents don't get to see their grandchildren at all.

2. It doesn't take more than 15 seconds to say "I love you!"

3. He said back to me, "I love you, too!"

4. A child had a whole parade just for him!

5. The police were there for a good reason!

6. There are creative ways to celebrate instead of not celebrating at all!

7. I have a car I could get there in!

8. I have money to buy gas for the car!

9. So many people showed up for the parade!

10. I didn't have to eat the obligatory piece of overly sweet birthday cake!

11. I gave him a gift!

12. The rain didn't start until the very end of the parade!

13. He has family and friends who care about him and love him deeply!

14. He's healthy!

15. Pandemics cannot cancel joy!

16. I made it home without having to stop at a public restroom—and I had to go REALLY badly through the whole thing!

17. #16 is worth repeating!

18. So much love was shown that evening!

That night, even in the midst of sadness, gratitude was my primary emotion. Gratitude begot joy, happiness, peace, thankfulness, mindfulness of the goodness in the world, and a sense of the Divine in a child's birthday parade.

Gratitude is not only the greatest of virtues but the parent of all others.

Is Anything Impossible?

"If you think nothing is impossible, try
slamming a revolving door."
—Anonymous[2]

My son and I have gone round and round on the topic of whether all things are possible. (No pun intended with the revolving door image.) A current popular mindset is that *anything* is possible if one believes one can do it—a "never say never" attitude. This is the position my son takes when he and I replay this conversation.

My position is that there are myriads of things I and many people cannot do, and it takes maturity to admit this with grace. As I point out to my son every time we traverse this well-worn path, I am an upper-middle-aged woman, and I am never going to be an Olympic gold-medal pole vaulter. Just ain't gonna happen.

He predictably responds that were I to pursue pole vaulting, I may not become an Olympic gold-medal winner, but by pursuing it at all, I may find that I have a facility for writing about sports and win a medal for reporting—which would never have happened had I not initially pursued the sport of pole vaulting.

Predictably I respond that a medal for writing about jumping 15 feet in the air is not the same thing as actually jumping 15 feet in the air . . .

to which he responds that closing the door on any idea prevents the birth of very doable ideas which may indeed lead to new life paths otherwise not considered . . .

to which I reply that I have no interest in either writing about nor actually doing pole vaulting because I can't do either one . . .

to which he replies, maybe not in this lifetime, but closing the door and saying "I can't" may prevent exploration of possible avenues both in this life and in the next lifetime because of the "I can't" mindset . . .

to which I reply: *sigh.* Whatever.

The problem with our well-rehearsed conversation is that we're each making a different, yet valid, point. He's absolutely correct that an "I can't" mindset on any one thing closes more than that one particular door. The "I can't" mindset is a slippery slope, making it easier to say "I can't" to things which "I actually can," but because the "I can't" mindset is set in my mind, I don't give new possibilities a chance to emerge.

I am absolutely correct that in this lifetime, I'm not going to be a gold medal Olympic pole vaulter. Nor am I going to win a Nobel prize for advanced mathematics in quantum physics . . .

to which he would respond, but you could read a quantum physics book for beginners to at least get an understanding of new paradigms . . .

OK, we're back to arguing two different points. My position is that there are physical and intellectual limitations present in every human being; acknowledge that with wisdom, maturity, and grace.

His position is that closing doors on one thing closes doors on multiple possibilities heretofore unthought of.

We're both right . . .

but I'm sure I would win the argument that it is impossible to slam a revolving door. I'm going to bring that up the next time we engage in this topic—to which I'm sure he will respond . . . but it *is* possible if one thinks ahead and adjusts the hydraulic system or preplaces a wedge in one of the revolving spokes of the door . . . to which I will respond: AARRG! *sigh.* Whatever.

Just Sit There

"Don't just do something, sit there!"
—Thich Nhat Hanh[3]

Oh, boy. For those who grew up with the Protestant work ethic; for those who had a grandmother who taught: "Do not rest until all your work is done;" for those who had a teacher who said, "You're not worth anything unless you are doing something productive"—boy, oh, boy. Nhat Hanh's quote is counter to our basic learnings.

Thich Nhat Hanh advocates sitting for the sake of sitting—not for the sake of resting; not for the sake of meditation; not for the sake of a quiet moment to think. Thich Nhat Hanh advocates sitting for no other reason than to sit—and to be mindful that we are sitting while we are sitting.

Nhat Hanh says that humankind's survival depends on our ability to stop rushing, that we have more than enough bombs and arms to destroy the world many times over, and yet we rush to make more. Unless we stop for a moment and simply sit—simply **_be_**—we'll remain under the illusion that we don't have enough, that we're not secure, that we must continuously fight our enemies . . . and the angst spawned from those thoughts spawns unhealthy, unpeaceful actions.

Sitting to simply sit allows the realization that we have enough, that life is good. When we stop long enough to experience this goodness, we can be nothing less than grateful. And when we are grateful, we are happy and at peace.

Can you sit for 15 *seconds* without filling your mind with thoughts of this, that, and the other thing? Give it a try. 15 *seconds*. If you're so busy that you don't have 15 *seconds* to sit in peace and gratitude, then you've just proven Thich Nhat Hanh's point! 15 *seconds*. Just sit, mindful that you are sitting. Do this often enough, and you will see the world in a radically new and wonderful way. 15 *seconds*.

How Much Guilt is Enough?

"How much guilt is enough? . . . When we
really examine it, we will always find that we
have been punishing ourselves for ignorance,
naivete, and lack of inner education."
—David R. Hawkins[4]

IMHO (text-speak for "in my humble opinion"), there is a place for guilt but not for shame. Let me explain.

Shame is a feeling of humiliation and unworthiness. It may or may not be related to a specific event.

Guilt is a feeling of remorse relating to a specific event.

Basically: Guilt admits *I did something wrong*. Shame believes *I am a worthless person*.

No matter how guilty someone may be, no person is worthless. Shame provides no redeeming qualities in the healing and correction processes. There is, however, a place for guilt.

Sociopaths never feel guilt. Therefore, a healthy mind and spirit knows when an act was dishonorable or uncharitable or hurtful, and the healthy mind and spirit feels guilt, feels remorse. That's how we know not to do the dishonorable act again.

Having said that, how much guilt is enough? Some persons hold onto remorse for the rest of their lives, punishing themselves with shame. I am not a psychologist, psychiatrist, counselor, or thera- pist; I have, however, over the years, come to the same realization that Dr. Hawkins expresses: when examined, the "wrongful" act was committed out of ignorance. If one had known the negative consequences beforehand; if one had more information to make a more informed decision; if one weren't desperate in a desperate situation . . . one would not have acted in the way one did.

Therefore, "enough guilt" is when one realizes the hurt and neg- ative consequences the specific act generated. When the con- sequences are realized, the lesson is learned. When the lesson is learned, it's time to let go of guilt, and the mature spirit would even give thanks to the Karma-Meister for the opportunity to have learned and developed as a person. (Of course, make amends when possible. "I apologize for my behavior" goes a long way in restoring relationships.)

However, nowhere in the aftermath of the "wrongful deed" is there a place for shame. No person is worthless, even when she makes poor-consequence choices. Feel the remorse, learn the lesson, make amends if possible, give thanks for the lesson, release the guilt.

When I was six years old in first grade, several of us first-graders were at a table coloring pictures. There was one box of eight large crayons for the group to share. I was using the red crayon, and I accidentally broke the group's red crayon! The other kids gave me the stink-eye. I felt shame, deep soul-searing shame. I've moved beyond the shame but have lived with guilt since then. Maybe it's time to let that guilt go. Will let you know when I do.

Do You Qualify to Cast the First Stone?

"If any of you have never sinned, then go
ahead and throw the first stone at her!"
—Jesus[5]

Some Christian faith traditions teach that sin is a stain on the human condition, that every person is born in sin. If that is your understanding of sin, then obviously you don't get to cast a stone at someone else because you're just as tainted.

Another understanding of sin is "bad or wrongful thoughts and actions." If that is your understanding of sin, then obviously you don't get to cast a stone because every human being has had uncharitable thoughts and done some actions that were not for the highest good of all. Nope, you don't get to throw a stone at someone if "bad or wrongful thoughts and actions" is your definition of sin.

I have heard sin described as "broken relationship." If that is your understanding of sin, then you don't get to even toss a stone at someone because no person has ever existed who got along with *every* person all the time. Nope, no stone-tossing for you.

My personal understanding of sin is "the illusion of separateness." In reality, we are One-in-the-Spirit; we're all interconnected with one another, we're all interconnected with nature, we're all interconnected with The Source of All Being. There is no such thing as non-connected or unconnectedness—except we live as though there is. We see another person as an "other," distinct from our own beingness; we see creation as something to exploit for her resources just to make our lives more convenient; we see those with different ideologies as enemies . . .

. . . except we're _not_ unconnected from others, creation, and "enemies." What one person does affects all of creation because of our interconnectedness; but we live as though this isn't true— and that's my understanding of sin: "the illusion of separateness."

If that is your definition of sin—the illusion of separateness—then you don't get to hurl a stone at someone else because spiritually, it's hurling a stone at yourself. Nope, no stone-hurling for those with this definition of sin.

So why all the judgment against others who "sin"? Because it lets us feel superior; allows us to feel that our sin is of a lesser degree, or of a more acceptable nature, or is more understand-able because of our circumstances. We judge others to let ourselves off the hook so we can feel better about ourselves at another's expense. Hmmm. Wonder what Jesus, Buddha, Muhammad (PBUH), Krishna, the Torah, Brahman would say about that rationalization—probably something like _Don't judge others just because they sin differently than you do._

INTERCONNECTEDNESS

"Man did not weave the web of life, he is merely a
strand in it. Whatever he does to the web, he does
to himself. One thing we know: our god is also
your god. The earth is precious to him and to harm
the earth is to heap contempt on its creator."

*"We do not inherit the earth from our ancestors;
we borrow it from our children."*
—Chief Seattle[6]

If I could choose one sentiment for all people to embrace from the indigenous peoples, it would be their understanding of interconnectedness with the earth.

So much harm has come to our Mother Earth (Gaia) in the name of progress; so much damage from greed; so much ravage and ruin from a misinterpretation of Genesis 1:28: *God blessed [humankind], and God said to them, "Be fruitful and multiply, and fill the earth and subdue it; and have dominion over the fish of the sea and over the birds of the air and over every living thing that moves upon the earth."*[7]

The first words God says to the humans are about their relationship to the earth; God bestows upon us some power (dominion) to take care of creation. By creating us in God's own image, God's intention for humans is to live in ways that emulate the characteristics of God. Humans are instructed to relate to nonhumans as God relates to them. A good ruler protects, not takes, from his subjects; a good protector has dominion, not domination, over her subjects...

...so let's look at the word *subdue*. Subdue means to bring something under control, to restrain, to overcome—as in subdue the enemy...but there are no enemies here, just the newly created earth. God's command to *subdue* the earth does not mean "see the earth as your enemy;" it means cultivate the earth in ways which honor the image and character of God—and that was a difficult task in those days. Farmers had to subdue the soil in order to till it; shelters had to be built to subdue wind and rain so that wind and rain wouldn't subdue humans. In Genesis chapter one, God shares divine power with humans so humans could relate to the earth and its inhabitants—human and non-human—in the ways that God relates to humans and non-humans. Humans are granted authority to tend this creation that God has called *good.*

The earth is precious to [God] and to harm the earth is to heap contempt on its creator.

And for those who prefer to understand ideas without a theological slant, then look at Chief Seattle's second quote from above: **We do not inherit the earth from our ancestors; we borrow it from our children.**

Why would we want to bequeath to our children and our children's children polluted rivers and toxic soil?

Whether one prefers a God-based understanding of creation and our role in it, or whether one prefers a secular understanding of nature and our place in it—either way, it's about *relationship* with creation/nature and our responsibility to bequeath a healthy earth to our descendants.

Individuals can do little things to help heal the earth (reduce, reuse, repurpose, recycle, etc.), but it's up to humanity as a whole to say to industry: STOP POLLUTING! Consider supporting legislation that prohibits raping the earth, or refrain from purchasing products from companies that are not eco-friendly. It's going to take a while to heal what we've harmed, but taking a tiny step forward towards healing is better than not taking a tiny step forward towards healing.

FOLLOW YOUR OWN PATH

"Never follow anyone else's path. Unless you're
in the woods and you're lost and you see a
path. Then by all means follow that path."
—Ellen DeGeneres[8]

Not everyone is a trailblazer, but we are all on our own path. That's important to remember when friends and family try to influence us. Sometimes the influence is helpful, sometimes it's not. When friends and family promote bigotry, prejudice, even hatred against others, then it's vital to remember we're on our own path and not under obligation to embrace the negativity that others (even our loved ones) embrace.

Sometimes parents want their kids to follow the path that they—the parents—have designed for them. A dad who was a high school football player wants his son to go pro—whether the son wants to or not. Or the mom-and-pop business owners expect their kids to carry on the business—whether the kids want to or not. Or lawyers expect their kid to be a lawyer, etc. etc. etc.

Those are not healthy paths for kids to follow if they don't want to do those things. We're all on our own path, and sometimes parents, significant others, family, friends forget that someone else's path is not theirs to direct.

Having said that, no person lives in a vacuum. Our choices affect others, and it's important to ensure that our choices don't actually harm others. For example, if you feel called to be a serial killer, it would behoove all if you did not follow that lifepath choice. But if you want to be a librarian instead of a school teacher as your mother, grandmother, and great-grandmother were, then be a librarian. Period.

A good guideline to ask yourself is if your lifepath choices have helped others along the way. If how one makes money involves some shady gray ethics, then revisiting the merits of that choice would be in order.

If one is in a career that someone else has chosen for him, then revisiting the pluses and minuses of said choice would be emotionally beneficial.

We cannot help but walk in the footsteps of our ancestors, and it is of great benefit to learn from their successes and failures. Nonetheless, we are on our own path.

If you are lost and you see a path of light leading out of the darkness, by all means take it . . . until you can find your own way again.

NEED V WANT . . . WITH A COUPLE OF CONCESSIONS

"With time, we have become increasingly
familiar with the concept of forced wants and
unfamiliar with the concept of basic needs."
—Rajesh Khanna[9]

Advertising has duped us into thinking we **_need_** this, that, and a bigger one of those. But think about it: what do we really **_need_**? We **_need_** shelter, food, clean water, several changes of clothes, and a pair of shoes. That's what we **_need_** to survive physically. Now take a look around and see what you have. I guarantee it's more than you **_need_**.

First concession: In our culture, it's difficult to get by without a phone, computer, and car. Granted. But we still have way more than we **_need_**.

If one wishes to step onto a soap box, one could point a condemning finger at the consumeristic, materialistic, worshipers-of-the-Almighty-Dollar marketing companies, claiming it's their fault that I want more, more, more because they tricked me into thinking I **_need_** the new gadget.

While marketing companies certainly play a role in western consumerism, that's not the soap box I think needs stepping on. In my opinion, the problem lies with the consumer's obliviousness to want versus need. Generally speaking, consumers are not mindful of need-versus-want when shopping; generally speaking, consumers are not mindful of an item's place of origin (sweatshops); and generally speaking, consumers are not aware of what natural resources were required to make a product (petroleum-based plastic, for example).

In my opinion, the greater onus lies with the *consumer* to make informed choices. Blaming marketing companies and greedy CEOs for society's insatiable desire for more is not where the problem of excess first arises—it's the consumer's non-mindful purchases.

Second concession: It's darn difficult to research a product. Even good Googlers have difficulty finding information on fair wages, for example, for all the steps along a product's journey from beginning to end; it's darn difficult to research where the ore was mined for said product and what damage was done to the earth to get said ore. Granted.

Nonetheless, mindfulness of whether a product is fair-trade or not is doable; mindfulness of a product's country of origin is relatively doable. It gets tricky because *everything* made in China is not made in sweatshops, just as *everything* made in the U.S. is not made by employees paid a living wage. Still, a small degree of mindfulness is better than no degree of mindfulness when purchasing something.

But the biggest non-mindfulness issue lies in confusing want with need. As Gandhi so eloquently put it, *Live simply so others may simply live*. If you really want the 5G thing, by all means get it and enjoy it! Just be mindful that it is a *want*, and do what you can to determine what wages and resources went into producing this *want*, and be mindful how many *wants* you are purchasing just to "keep up with the Joneses."

A bit of consumer-mindfulness goes a long way, and marketing companies will note well if enough consumers back off from an excess of *want*-shopping and begin purchasing products that support living wages, fair-trade, and noting the effects on the environment the production of said product incurred.

It's not totally up to the marketing companies to change the consumerism plague of our society. It's also up to the consumer, and that's you and me.

LABELS. HUMPH.

"There is no such thing as a pure introvert or extrovert.
Such a person would be in the lunatic asylum."
—Carl Jung[10]

Jung himself coined the labels *introvert* and *extrovert*, and Jung himself said there's no person who is 100% introverted or extroverted. We are all, to use another Jungian term, *ambivert*.

Labels can be a useful tool if used to describe predominant characteristics; it facilitates conversation so we don't have to use 759 words to describe particular characteristics each time we want to reference them.

BIG PROBLEM: People tend to label other people as though that one label defines the person in-toto. According to Jung, no person is 100% any label.

In general, I tend to be a tree-hugging-embrace-the-woo-woo type of person. But there are particulars in which I am quite conservative. I am bluish-purple flowers hanging on a bright green tree.

And if I were a betting woman—and I am—I'd bet that those who are labeled or even self-labeled as staunch conservatives have a couple of light blue polka dots with some light green spots somewhere in their philosophies of life.

It frustrates me when groups of people are labeled. Betcha I can find more than one of "those people" who are not anything like "the label," and even if they have some characteristics of the label, no one is 100% any label.

Make no mistake: labels have their place. I appreciate labels because they let me know that this can contains green beans and that can contains creamed corn. Those labels are very useful indeed.

But to label someone implies that that person is that thing and nothing more . . . humph. Even Jung said no person is 100% anything.

Although, could it be argued that I am (and all people are) 100% a conglomeration of things? I can imagine myself posing this question to Dr. Jung; I can also imagine Dr. Jung replying "Audrey, you are 100% annoying!" Well, Dr. Jung, you wouldn't be the first to label me as that!

Labels tend to be more inaccurate than accurate—which says more about the one labeling than the one labeled. Just sayin'.

PEACE TAKES BOTH HOLDING ON AND LETTING GO

"What would we have to hold in compassion
to be at peace right now? What would we have
to let go of to be at peace right now?"
—Jack Kornfield[11]

Only you know the answer to that.

~~~~~~

WHAT IF . . .

"Whenever I hear anyone arguing for slavery, I feel
a strong impulse to see it tried on him personally."
—Abraham Lincoln[12]

Abe Lincoln gave voice to a specific sentiment that I hold in general. When I hear someone complaining about someone else, I want to say, "Would you like to trade lives with them? If not, then hush-up about 'em!"

As Lincoln implies, only not-slaves argued for slavery.

Let's play a what-if game. The first question is based on Lincoln's quote.

What if . . .

those who argued for slavery had to first be a slave for 20 years?

What if . . .

Congress had to live on the current minimum wage without access to any other income? (How long do you predict it would take for the minimum wage to rise?)

What if . . .

there really is reincarnation and you had to come back as a member of the group you negatively judged in this life (be it gays,

Blacks, Whites, Middle-Easterners, border-crossers without documentation, the unemployed, etc.)

What if . . .

you had to watch from the other side of the veil how generations from now had to live in the pollution we created and didn't clean up?

What if . . .

you had to switch places with the person with whom you hold a grudge? How would you like to be on the receiving end of your grudginess?

What if . . .

you could actually see into the soul of another, and you saw how your words affected him? (You could see how your compliment lifted his feeling of self-worth; you could see how telling a child she sings well inspired her career; you could see how your well-intentioned suggestion came off as a criticism because of your voice tone; you could see that if you had apologized, the relationship would have been restored . . .)

What if . . .

conversations focused on satisfying the interests of each side instead of fighting to defend positions?

What if . . .

we re-learned how to disagree partially instead of disagreeing totally because of a single issue?

What if . . .

we were able to see why desperate people do desperate things? (Would we reconstruct society so that situations never became desperate for anyone?)

Sometimes the first step towards transformation is to ask "what if."

~~~~~~

BE POSITIVE INSTEAD OF NOT-NEGATIVE.

"I will never attend an anti-war rally; when
you have a peace rally, invite me."
—Mother Teresa[13]

Mother Teresa understood the benefits of being *for* something instead of *against* something. One of the issues with protestors and politicians is that they are almost always *against* something. This just puts out more negative energy.

Let's express what we *do* want, what we'd prefer the world to be like. Let's give voice to what resolution we want rather than list the results we don't want.

For example: "I'd like better health" rather than "I don't want to be sick."

"I don't want to be sick" has two negatives ("don't" and "sick"). In mathematics, two negatives make a positive. In the realm of vibrations, two negatives make twice as many negative vibrations.

To reference Mother Teresa's quote: "I want a peaceful world" expresses what she wants; "I don't want war" has two negatives ("don't" and "war"). Why is this important? Because "not war" is not the same as "peace." "Not war" could mean just a temporary lull in overt violence; "peace" (or a more inclusive word is *shalom*) means safety and security and justice for all.

If we learn to express what we want, what we're *for*, then we help heal the world with positive energy—or for those of us who grew up in the 70s: *good vibrations*!

You get the idea. Projecting good vibrations into the world is groovy, man!

~~~~~~

GRATITUDE

"If the only prayer you ever say in your entire
life is thank you, it will be enough."
—Meister Eckhart[14]

Gratitude acknowledges the goodness present, goodness that we may otherwise overlook because of the day's problems. Gratitude begets compassion and empathy. Gratitude orients the focus on what's right instead of what's wrong; what we have instead of what we lack. Gratitude raises one's spiritual vibrations.

Anne Lamott[15] says there are three kinds of prayer:

- Help me.

- Thank you.

- Wow!

"Help me" prayers are, I'm guessing, the most common prayer, and by all means, continue petitioning The Source of All Blessings for help when needed.

But what if we had a friend who, *every time* we talked with her, did nothing but ask for help. Wouldn't that get annoying?

"Wow!" prayers are an acknowledgement that there is something greater than oneself at play in the dynamics of the universe. But here's the slippery slope of "Wow!" prayers: they have the potential to focus on the event rather than the Power behind the event.

If one experiences a "miracle," (and we'll talk about what a miracle is in just a moment)—if one experiences a miracle, our initial response might be "WOW!" But that is focusing on the finger pointing to the moon instead of on the moon itself. <u>The Power behind the miracle is the actual WOW!</u> —not the amazing event itself.

The deepest response to *any*thing in life is *Thank you!* "Thank you" as the response for the smallest gifts to the largest "miracles" acknowledges one's place before the ineffable PRESENCE. "Thank you" shows appreciation for the goodness that surrounds life itself.

OK, so what is a *miracle*? My definition of a miracle is anything that brings a deeper awareness of God. (If the word "God" is a turnoff for you, then substitute a word or phrase that is meaningful to you: PRESENCE; The Divine; Source; Spirit; The Ground of All Being-ness . . . I don't want to get bogged down right now on the baggage associated with the word "God.")

A blade of grass is a miracle if one becomes more deeply aware of the Divine-Spirit-PRESENCE within that blade of grass.

The birth of a baby is a miracle if one becomes more deeply aware of the Source-Of-All-Being's vibrations within the birthing process and the child.

A piece of paper is a miracle. Think about it: the paper is made from a tree. A tree has within it sunlight, moonlight, starlight, rain, nutrients from the soil in which it grew. The tree has within it the energy of critters who once had a home in it. The piece of paper has within it those who timbered the wood, hauled the wood, pulped the wood, formed the wood pulp into paper, those who packaged the paper, and those who trucked the paper to distribute it for sale.

A single piece of paper contains elements of the entire universe!

How do we not say thank you for the miracle of a piece of paper!

Consider this: Upon waking, say "Thank you, Divine Spirit! What a marvelous and miraculous day you have given me!"

Upon retiring for bed, say, "Thank you, Divine Spirit! What a marvelous and miraculous day you have given me!"

We're not really saying thank you for any specific event of the day—and some specific events would be really difficult to say thank you for—we're saying thank you to the PRESENCE behind, within, around, and through the day.

<u>Gratitude is not so much an emotion as *a way of being, a way of living.*</u>

"If the only prayer you ever say in your entire life is thank you, it will be enough."

DEFINERS DON'T DEFINE UNLESS YOU LET THEM.

"Definitions belong to the definers, not the defined."
—Toni Morrison[16]

If someone calls you stupid, that says absolutely <u>nothing</u> about you; all it says is that the person saying it thinks you're stupid.

If someone calls you beautiful, that says absolutely <u>nothing</u> about you; all it says is that the person saying it thinks you're beautiful.

If someone calls you stubborn, that says absolutely <u>nothing</u> about you; all it says is that the person saying it thinks you're stubborn.

If someone calls you witty, that says absolutely <u>nothing</u> about you; all it says is that the person saying it thinks you're witty.

Why, then, do we get upset when someone defines us as stupid and stubborn (or feel good when defined as beautiful and witty)? Because there is a tiny piece of us that believes him.

If someone described you as 20 feet tall, you wouldn't believe her because there isn't even a smidgen of you that believes you're 20 feet tall.

God has defined you as beloved. That's the only absolute definition of you that is always true. Let's live as though we believe that and let go of any human's opinion.

HOPE V WISH

"May your choices reflect your hopes, not your fears."
—Nelson Mandela[17]

Let's start by differentiating between hopes and wishes.

A hope has some degree of expectation that a desired result could occur.

A wish may or may not have a degree of expectation that a desired result could occur.

I might wish I looked like Dolly Parton, but even with enhancement of specific parts, I'm still not going to look like Dolly Parton. There's zero degree of expectation of this desired result.

Hope, unlike wishes, *always* has some degree of expectation that a desired result could occur, otherwise the desire is nothing more than a wish.

I hope for world peace. While there is little chance this will happen in my lifetime, there's still a chance. I hope to win the lottery; the odds are infinitesimal, but there's still a chance.

There's another difference between hope and wish: Hope has an unspoken assumption beneath the surface that a power greater than oneself plays a part in the dynamics of manifestation. There are steps one can take to help manifest the hope, but at some point, we need to surrender the outcome.

"I hope for world peace." Yes, there are small things I can do to contribute to this outcome, but for world peace to happen, powers greater than myself will have to contribute.

"I hope everyone gets home safely from the party." I can do only so much for this desired outcome. I can ensure no one drives impaired; I can allow guests to stay longer if the weather is inclement . . . but other than that, "all guests getting home safely" is out of my hands.

Now let's apply this understanding of hope to Mandela's quote: *May your choices reflect your hopes, not your fears.*

We make choices every day. I choose to lock my doors at night, *not* out of fear but out of hope for a safe night's sleep.

I choose to wear a seatbelt, *not* out of fear but out of hope for safe travels.

I choose to financially support non-profit organizations that work for healing the environment, *not* out of fear but out of hope for a better tomorrow.

We make choices every day. Choices grounded in fear yield fear-based results; choices grounded in hope yield hopeful results. We need to do our part for our hopes to be realized and then let the power greater than ourselves do its part.

ANGER IS A SIGN OF HURT FEELINGS

"The strong is not the one who is physically powerful,
but indeed, the one who controls himself when angry."
—Muhammad (PBUH)[18]

Why do we get angry? Psychology 101 says that anger is a secondary emotion, meaning that another emotion came first; but expressing that underlying emotion is too painful, so we conjure up anger to hide the primary emotion . . . which is usually some form of hurt feelings.

So what hurts our feelings? Psychologists would say that the ego feels threatened.

OK, so what threatens the ego? Insecurity that there is a grain of truth in what the other has said about us; not feeling heard; feeling disrespected; frustration; unfairness.

All those things that threaten the ego feel legitimate in the heat of the moment, and let's say they are. Let's say someone is *not* respecting you; someone is *not* listening to understand your point of view. Feeling hurt would be quite understandable, but lashing back in anger isn't conducive to resolution or relationship.

Sometimes anger comes from feeling stressed about a non-related issue; for example, if someone has chronic financial issues, the on-going stress of that keeps one "on edge" so that when the customer relations agent can't figure out why you were charged double, we get angry at him—except we're not really angry at the customer relations agent; we're angry that we have chronic financial issues, and being charged double increases the stress, and the stress is producing adrenalin and cortisone and a bunch of other medical words I don't understand which are, nonetheless, affecting our physiology which makes us angry—and the incompetent clerk is an easy target to vent at.

What to do about that?

If possible, identify what triggers the anger. That's difficult to do in the heat of the moment, so after the rawness abates, think honestly about what triggered it. Is it that you really are deep-down concerned that what the person said about you had some merit? Are you actually chronically stressed about finances? Think about this honestly when not angry. (It won't be fun. Do it anyway.)

The old adage of counting-to-ten before speaking has some merit. It buys time so that the first words blurted aren't cruel-back-in-your-face-regrettable words. Experience has taught me, though, that counting to 10 usually doesn't buy enough time. If possible, walk away for a while. Granted that's not always possible, but when possible, walk away until a more rational frame of mind can be acquired.

Did you know that the physical body cannot be angry and distance-run at the same time? True—except what good does that do for those of us who can't distance-run! Any form of exercise will help dissipate the immediate anger. I remember one time I was so angry with someone, that I went for a walk in bitter cold weather with ice pellets hitting my face. For the first mile, I was so angry that I didn't notice the cold and ice pellets; then, after another half-mile, the anger abated and I *very much* noticed the cold and ice pellets! Darn. Gotta walk a mile and a half back home in the stupid cold and ice pellets. When I got back home, I was still upset about the situation, but the raw anger gave way to just trying to warm up.

For more information on how to address anger, check out the myriad of self-help books available; a quick Google search will yield helpful tips. And if anger becomes the controlling force more often than not, please get professional help.

The problem is not that we get angry. <u>The problem is when we can't control the anger</u>—*when the anger controls us*—and we lash back out-of-control. That's indeed a problem. Muhammad (PBUH) reminds us that it takes inner strength to control oneself when angry. Think about this the next time your fast-food order is wrong *again*.

HUH?

"A careful analysis of the process of observation in atomic physics has shown that the subatomic particles have no meaning as isolated entities, but can only be understood as interconnections between the preparation of an experiment and the subsequent measurement."
—Erwin Schrodinger[19]

I have no idea what this means.

P.S. It shows wisdom to know when *not* to speak.

SCIENCE V RELIGION

"For small creatures such as we, the vastness
is bearable only through love."
—Carl Sagan[20]

Science and religion have been at war for a very long time. In my opinion, they are complimentary, not contradictory. The problem is that each side has alienated the other with claims of superiority instead of affording respect for what the other offers that each side on its own, can't.

The institutional church has historically poo-pooed science, claiming that God is the only force in the universe that causes things to happen, and to ascribe any kind of meaning other than God to natural events is heresy at best, blasphemy at worst.

This understanding of the natural universe might have been understandable 10,000 years ago. Since then, we have discovered stuff like gravity and heliocentrism. It took the institutional church 359 years to admit this. No wonder science has washed its hands of organized religion. What religion is missing is humility.

Religion, on the other hand, has some valid points, too. Science, without a conscience, is cold. Science has no moral imperative to feed the hungry. Science has developed gadgets and technologies that are potentially harmful for humankind's evolution. What science is missing is humility.

Religion without science can devolve into superstition; science without religion is unconcerned with moral imperatives and with misuse of discoveries. As Bob Proctor so eloquently puts it: *You can cook a man's dinner with electricity, and you can also cook the man.*

Science can trace the Big Bang's history to less than a second before the actual bang, but science cannot explain why the bang happened at all. It's a mystery. Religion acknowledges the mystery, then hides behind it without using the intellect to explore and understand the wondrous nature of the universe.

OBVIOUSLY—the above statements are stereotypes of science and religion at their extremes. Granted. The point of the above statements is to illustrate with a limited number of words some of the reasons science and religion have traditionally not played well together. Both claim supremacy in explaining that which ultimately cannot be explained fully. Both disclaim the merits of the other. Both lack *humility* in relationship with the other.

Carl Sagan's quote is one step towards bridging the science v religion divide. While Sagan may not equate the word *love* with God, religion does. One of the most ancient and descriptive names for God is *Love*. Love is an energy that cannot be explained by science. While such things as EEGs are crucial to understanding brain function and diagnoses of disease, produce all the EEG data ya want and we'll still never understand why love transcends differences, why love unites, why love heals. We'll never understand why love exists in the first place, much less the ultimate Source of it. Love is a mystery, and it is a mystery that science will never "solve."

When science embraces *love* as a beneficial unifying, mysterious force, then science and religion have taken a leap towards complimenting each other. When religion acknowledges that the Prime Mover created a creation that keeps on *evolving*, then science and religion have taken a leap towards mutual respect.

When religion understands the biblical creation stories as mythical poetry, and when science quits naming things "the God particle," then maybe science and religion can better dialogue with each other.

When science and religion stand hand in hand at the Grand Canyon and simultaneously say *WOW! We stand in gratitude for the Power behind the power of this evolutionary beauty*—well, gosh. Maybe then science and religion can learn to play well together after all.

~~~~~~

LUCK?

"Luck never made a man wise."
—Seneca[21]

My parents insisted I take four years of math in high school. They thought it would look good on transcripts submitted with college applications. I see their point, but after one semester of high school freshman math, I was, shall we say, lost.

Junior year was trigonometry. From day one, I didn't understand what the teacher was talking about. Midway through the course, the teacher told the class to do problem #7. To give the illusion that I had an inkling of how to even start problem #7, I put some numbers on my paper and came up with an answer. (Any answer would do.)

I looked around, and all the smart kids were still working on it. Not a good sign. Tentatively I raised my hand to give my answer. What did I have to lose; wouldn't be the first time I gave a wrong answer in math class. The teacher called on me.

WOWZER! HOLY COW! My answer was correct!!!!!!!! I sat up a little straighter as the teacher went on with the lesson because I, math-challenged Audrey, got the correct trigonometry answer!

My best friend sat behind me; she was and is very good at math. She tapped me on the shoulder and whispered, "Let me see how you did that."

I leaned to the side so she could see my work. After a moment, she whispered, "I don't believe it. You did the wrong problem! You did problem #8, and you did it incorrectly. But your wrong answer to the wrong problem just happened to be the right answer to #7!"

I whispered back, "What's your point? I got the answer the teacher wanted and you didn't!"

I am living proof that there is indeed such a thing as luck! (And no, the point of this reflection is not that two wrongs make a right; not where I'm headed with this.)

More people lament how they're never lucky rather than celebrate how lucky they really are. Friends, there's such a thing as a self-fulfilling prophecy. Keep labeling yourself as unlucky, and those vibrations are going to attract more unluckiness; at the very least, an "I'm unlucky" mindset prevents one from noticing all the times one is lucky.

Some philosophers claim luck is nothing but preparation meeting opportunity, or that lucky people are the ones who take more chances and thereby have more opportunities for good things to happen.

Whether there's such a thing as "random" luck, or whether Clotho, Lachesis, and Atropos (the three Fates in Greek mythology) determine who does and who doesn't receive luck, or whether karma determines the manifestations in any given moment—I have no idea.

Maybe luck never made a man wise, but it sure got me through one day of high school trigonometry! To this day I consider myself lucky. Maybe a bit of "luck" will come your way if you stop considering yourself unlucky and start telling yourself that you are indeed lucky. Just see what happens over time. I make no promises on behalf of the Universe, the Greek mythological Fates, or the Karma-Meister. But considering oneself lucky is bound to bring better results than walking through life believing oneself to be unlucky. Give it a try. Tell yourself you're lucky and see what manifests over time.

FALL, GET UP;
FALL AGAIN, GET UP AGAIN

"The real test is not whether you avoid failure, because
you won't. It's whether you let it harden or shame
you into inaction, or whether you learn from it."
—Barak Obama[22]

Confucius says: "Our greatest glory is not in never falling but in rising every time we fall."[23]

One-year-olds grasp this intuitively. When learning to walk, toddlers fall down every other step . . . and get back up every other step without thinking, "I'll never do this; I give up."

Bottom line: We are going to fall and fail, and not all falls and fails are physical. One of Thomas Edison's teachers told him he was "too stupid to learn anything." He got up from that verbal fall and eventually invented the light bulb. Granted, it took 1000 tries for Edison to get the light bulb to work, and when asked why he didn't give up after failing so many times, Edison replied, "I have not failed. I've just found ten thousand ways that won't work."[24]

Both Obama and Confucius say that it's not about avoiding falls and failure; it's about getting up *when* we fall or fail. Maybe there will be a time when we can't get up from a fall or failure by ourselves; then get help and do what you can from this new starting point.

Do we let our falls and fails harden and shame, or do we learn and persevere?

Ask a one-year-old for the answer.

~~~~~~

THINK ABOUT THINKING ABOUT IT

"Ignorance, the root and stem of every evil."
—Plato[25]

Well that's very Buddhist of Plato!

One of the main precepts of Buddhism is that *ignorance* is the root of suffering. One of the main precepts of Plato is that *ignorance* is the root of evil.

Interesting that Plato and Buddha lived roughly around the same time, and both, without the other's knowledge, identified <u>ignorance</u> as the root of some very not nice things.

Plato's philosophy emphasizes ignorance of what makes for a "good society," and Buddha's philosophy emphasizes ignorance in individuals' right-behavior. Individuals' <u>right-behavior creates a good society</u> of comprehensive well-being for all. It's the *"for all"* that stumbles individuals and societies. Ignorance of what "for all" actually means creates an *unjust* society for some.

Granted, that's quite a broad brushstroke to explain two intricate and profound ideologies, but ultimately, <u>both Plato and Buddha teach us to transcend ignorance</u>.

Booker T. Washington said, *"You can't hold a man down without staying down with him."*[26] While Mr. Washington is referring to one race oppressing another race (systemic racism), his quote holds broader truth from which individuals and societies can benefit:

- Countries "hold down" (occupy) other countries (for the sake of power and resources)

- Businesses "hold down" the lowest paid workers (because paying them more would affect the company's profits or—heaven forbid!—the CEO's salary)

- Religions "hold down" non-members of that religion either through spiritual terrorism (proselytizing with threat of hell) rather than with loving invitation; or with arrogance that "my way of understanding an unknowable God is better than your way of understanding an unknowable God"

- Individuals "hold down" other individuals for no reason than the other individual is different (supremacy mindset)

- Individuals refuse to understand any point of view but their own (superiority mindset)

All this "holding down" stems from ignorance.

We can't help what we are taught as children; we *can* help what ignorance we choose to hold onto as adults.

If one doesn't know any better, can one be excused from wrongful behavior? At first, yes, but there comes a point when adults need to take personal responsibility to transcend personal ignorance, to learn what causes suffering and evil, and to identify how they participate (usually unwittingly) in perpetuating the suffering and evil in society.

If one person transcends even a little bit of ignorance, we're one step closer to a good society *for all*. At least think about thinking about it.

FOCUS ON WHAT'S RIGHT

"Let us rise up and be thankful, for if we didn't learn
a lot today, at least we learned a little, and if we didn't
learn a little, at least we didn't get sick, and if we got
sick, at least we didn't die; so let us all be thankful."
—Buddha[27]

In any given day . . .

Oh how often we overlook the 9,999 things that went right and focus on the one thing that went wrong.

Oh how often we overlook the 999 things we possess and focus on the one thing we don't have.

Oh how often we overlook the 99 compliments we received and focus on the one uncharitable comment someone made.

Oh how often we say 9 prayers of "Help me, Lord" and say one prayer of gratitude.

Oh how much better life would be if we reversed those numbers.

LAUGHTER REALLY IS THE BEST MEDICINE

"The next time a stranger talks to you when you're alone,
just look at them shocked and whisper, 'You can see me?'"
—Anonymous[28]

When's the last time you had some good-natured *silly* fun? Most of us are way too busy being serious, telling others about our problems, worrying about the future.

It's a scientific fact[29] that laughter is a form of medicine. Laughter lowers stress, strengthens the immune system, lowers pain levels.

Buddhists have a laughter meditation for no other purpose than to laugh. The laughter is not from seeing or hearing something funny; rather, the laughter's source is within oneself. Check out some laughter meditations on YouTube. It's difficult not to laugh at them laughing!

Or watch a YouTube video of foxes laughing. It's hilarious! Truly I say unto thee: Thou hast not lived life to the fullest if thou hast not watched a video of foxes laughing!

Try standing in front of a mirror and laughing; you'll look so silly that you'll laugh at yourself laughing. (Seriously, try this. Do it when you're home alone so that you won't feel self-conscious.

Just stand in front of a mirror and laugh; it's the silliest thing to watch yourself laugh!)

So laugh and do something for no other reason than it's good-natured fun: set five of the silliest looking garden gnomes around the hedges in your front yard; goofy looking flamingos work well, too. Hang a birdhouse decorated in the funniest way; get some wacky tree decorations . . .

Laughter heals the body, mind, and soul. What medicine could possibly be better than laughing!

Knowledge + Compassion = Wisdom

"Yesterday I was clever, so I wanted to change the
world. Today I am wise, so I am changing myself."
—Rumi[30]

Clever means intelligent; quick to understand; knowledgeable.

Wise means showing good judgment by marrying knowledge with compassion.

One can be quite clever but not wise.

Wisdom means knowing when to give your opinion and when not to.

Wisdom means knowing how to make a point without poking.

Wisdom means knowing how to criticize injustice without criticizing people.

Wisdom means knowing that kindness is more important than niceness.

Wisdom means knowing that religion is not the same as experiencing the Divine.

Wisdom means knowing what's ultimately important and what's not.

Wisdom means knowing the difference between fact and opinion.

Wisdom means knowing there is always two sides to a story, and . . .

Wisdom means knowing that I don't know the full story of either side.

Wisdom means knowing that relationships are based on respect, not on being right.

Cleverness tries to change the world by changing other people; wisdom tries to change the world by changing oneself. If you want the world to be more peaceful, be more peaceful. If you want the world to be more forgiving, be more forgiving.

Intelligence has a place, an important place. More information is better than less information when making decisions. More information helps one discern what "facts" are true and what "facts" are slanted for political purposes.

But . . . all the knowledge in the world without compassion does not make the world a better place. Wisdom does.

LEARN, LEARN, LEARN

"Surround yourself with people who are smarter than you."
—Russell Simmons[31]

"Half of being smart is knowing
what you are dumb about."
—Solomon Short[32]

It wouldn't be much of a match if Michael Jordan and I played basketball together. He'd win, and he wouldn't learn a thing playing against me. I, on the other hand, might actually learn how to dribble a basketball.

Actors become better actors when they perform with seasoned actors.

Doctors become better doctors when they work with highly skilled professionals.

Lawyers become better lawyers when up against the best of the best.

The same holds true for our minds. Being around someone who knows more than you gives opportunity for insights you wouldn't think of on your own. Observing how someone smarter than you processes information raises *your* "performance level."

Unfortunately, some folks don't know that they are uninformed . . . because they haven't spent time with folks who are informed. They think the two facts they have are the whole story. That just leads to the propagation of misinformation.

Can you publicly admit you don't know something?

The benefit of surrounding yourself with people smarter than you is that it leads to a better version of yourself.

BE KIND ANYWAY

"Be kinder than necessary because everyone you
meet is fighting a battle you know nothing about."
—J.M. Barrie[33]

Being kind does not mean being a doormat; it does mean not being vindictive.

Being kind does not mean tolerating abuse; it does mean not being abusive back.

Being kind does not mean remaining silent in the face of injustice; it does mean speaking up respectfully.

Recall the difference between "nice" and "kind." "Nice" doesn't create waves; "kind" may very well create waves where inequity or disrespect exists, but "kind" *always* seeks the highest good.

You have no idea what I have been through in my life, and very few people know the emotional scars in my spirit, so please be kind to me.

I have no idea what you have been through in your life; I've no idea what caused your emotional scars, so I will do my best to be kind to you.

Now if we could hold that sentiment in place when the #$%^ driver cuts us off and when the *&^% clerk has no idea how to resolve my account; if we could hold that sentiment when we see . . . anyone! . . . then the world just might heal a little bit more each day.

~~~~~~

His Tone Is His Karma; How I Respond Is My Karma

"The trouble with most of us is that we would rather be ruined by praise than saved by criticism."
—Norman Vincent Peale[34]

Who wouldn't rather be ruined by praise than saved by criticism! Praise just feels better than having someone point out what I'm doing wrong, or worse, having someone point out what's wrong with me!

Here's the thing: praise is necessary so we know we've done a good job on something, but when we can't handle criticism, then we'll never get better at something, and even our friends will start tip-toeing on egg shells around us. That dynamic is awkward at best, relationship-losing at worst.

If the criticism is given in a well-meaning tone for the purpose of helping, then be honest with yourself if the criticism actually has merit. If so, then you've learned something for your betterment. If it doesn't have merit, then dismiss it.

If the criticism was given in a judgmental, even cruel, tone for the purpose of embarrassing, then be honest with yourself if the criticism actually has merit. If so, then you've learned something for your betterment. If it doesn't have merit, then dismiss it.

Note that our response to both well-meaning and cruel criticism is the same: Think about it. <u>The tone of someone's criticism is his karma; how we respond is our karma.</u>

An on-the-spot response I've found helpful when confronted with criticism is, "OK, I'll think about that. Thank you for telling me." This response lets the person know she was heard, and "thank you for telling me" puts an end to the conversation. If she continues, just keep repeating, "thank you for telling me." Eventually she'll stop if she gets no further response from you. Repeated for emphasis: <u>The tone of someone's criticism is his karma; how we respond is our karma.</u>

Don't let ego block you from thinking honestly about the criticism. Why would you sacrifice improvement just because someone implied you aren't perfect!

CHANGE IS THE NATURAL ORDER OF THINGS

"It may be hard for an egg to turn into a bird: it would be a jolly sight harder for it to learn to fly while remaining an egg. We are like eggs at present. And you cannot go on indefinitely being just an ordinary, decent egg. We must be hatched or go bad."
—C.S. Lewis[35]

Human beings are creatures of habit. It's easier *not* to change than to change. Perhaps that's because change requires work when we already have enough work with things just the way they are.

There's also a fear of the unknown, evoking the old saying, "Better the devil I know than the devil I don't know."

But as C.S. Lewis points out, if the egg doesn't change, it will rot. The seed has to change or it won't become a flower; the cocoon has to change or it won't become a butterfly.

Change is hardest when it's thrust upon us with no warning and when we don't have a say in what changes. Then it feels like a loss of control.

What I've found helpful is to intentionally change little things so that when big changes come, I'm already used to dealing with change. For example, when I dust the house, I intentionally set my knick-knacks in different places. Every few months I switch the compartments of my knives, forks, and spoons in the silver-ware tray. When reorganizing, I intentionally get rid of something, be it clothing, knick-knacks, books to make room for the new.

In other words, I *intentionally* change little things so that when *unintentional* change comes, I'm already used to dealing with change.

What is a small thing you can intentionally change in your home that prepares your spirit for when big changes come?

Everybody Is
Some Degree of Gray

"We must develop and maintain the capacity to forgive.
He who is devoid of the power to forgive is devoid of
the power to love. There is some good in the worst of
us and some evil in the best of us. When we discover
this, we are less prone to hate our enemies."
—Martin Luther King, Jr.[36]

Years ago, a teacher-friend told me that when the teachers in her school gathered in the teacher's lounge, and one of the teachers started griping about a student, the "rule" in the teacher's lounge was that for every negative comment the teacher made about a particular student, she had to name two good things about the student.

This is a marvelous way to keep from labeling particular students as "bad." There is no *totally* bad student, just as there is no *totally* perfect student.

That person you don't like, the one you hold a grudge against . . . what are two good things about her?

That person who is obnoxious, who holds obnoxious political views, who speaks obnoxiously, and there is no other word to describe the jerk other than "obnoxious" …what are two good things about him?

It's easier, for some reason, to come up with two negatives about our best friend, so we don't need to practice that; it's more difficult to come up with two positives about "that idiot." Even "that idiot" has some redeeming qualities, even if said qualities are buried deep. If the best you can come up with for one of the positive qualities is, "She has nice eyelashes," then let that suffice for the moment. Try again later for a bit more depth.

Yes, it's going to be hard to name two positive things about the hater; but how are we any different if we hate him back?

~~~~~~

RUACH

"What is God? [God] is the breath inside the breath."
—Kabir[37]

Kabir, an Indian mystic born in 1440, was revered by Hindus, Muslims, and Sikhs. In the above quote, Kabir speaks of breath within breath. The Hebrew word for breath is *ruach*.

Interesting, isn't it, how at their cores, religions that historically have been antagonistic towards each other are actually all pointing to the same thing: Oneness within the Sacred Eternal Spirit-ness.

Where do *you* experience God? Christians might say the church; Muslims, the mosque; Hindus and Buddhists, the temple; Jews, the synagogue; the non-churched might say family; Wicca, nature.

Of course God is in those places, but God is even closer than the closest church or mosque or temple or synagogue or family member or tree: God is the life-force within your breath. Wherever you are, God is not only there, God is within you.

There is no place God is not, *including in our breath*. Do we honor this divine breath (*ruach*) when we trash-talk; when we tell ethnic jokes; when we call someone an enemy—who has the exact same divineness in his breath as we have in ours?

God is the breath inside the breath; God is the life-force within your breath—*ruach*. Does being aware of this give you pause to choose your words a bit more reverently?

Small Things Make a Difference

"What you do makes a difference, and you have to decide what kind of difference you want to make."
—Jane Goodall[38]

Most of us will not make a difference big enough to merit a chapter in a history book; chances are, we won't be even a footnote in a history book . . . but that doesn't mean we can't change the course of history. Every act, no matter how small, changes how the world moves forward.

- When you wash the dishes with gratitude that you've had food, the world is a more *grateful* place.

- When you do a load of laundry cheerfully, the world is a more *cheerful* place.

- When you smile at someone, the world is a *gentler* place.

- When you take someone to a doctor's appointment, the world is a more *caring* place.

- When you remain hopeful that the Divine can transform personal and global turmoil, the world is a more *hopeful* place.

- When you challenge derogatory comments and do not tell or laugh at degrading jokes, the world is a more *just* place.

- When you take time to simply BE with the PRESENCE, the world is a more *peaceful* place.

None of those actions will get your name in a history book, but you change the course of history simply because you did a little thing with great love.

THERE'S NO PERSONAL GROWTH WITHOUT CHANGE

"Change is inevitable except from a vending machine."
—Robert C. Gallagher[39]

Mr. Gallagher is right. No need for mentation and metaphysical pondering. One is either going to get his change from a vending machine or not.

If nothing changed, it would not be possible for the mind to develop. If no external factor prompted some human to figure out how to add and subtract, why would the human mind bother with arithmetic; there had to be an external impetus to entice some human to add more of something to something and take away something from something else. Some external factor evoked the need to figure out how to add and subtract.

And without first learning addition and subtraction, humans would never have developed the ability to multiply and divide; if humans never learned to multiply and divide, humans would never have learned to find the cosecant in a triangle.

I've no idea what practical applications there are to knowing the cosecant, but maybe it's important in engineering or calculating the curvature of telescope lenses for astrobiology. No idea. (I admire cosecant-philes who actually know what a cosecant is ☺.)

Anyway, without external change, we could not change internally. For example, getting through middle school is one of the most life-changing chapters a person can experience. Coming out of middle school, one's character is either the stronger for it or scarred for life. Either way, one is changed mentally and emotionally (internally) from the external context.

Without those internally developmental middle-school years, we would be ill-prepared to handle the workplace because the workplace changes us, too.

One either finds a vocation that entrains the spirit to pleasing vibrations because the job is so fulfilling, or one trudges to work day after day only to notice one's spirit is calcifying due to the unpleasant idiots one has to deal with day after day. Either way, one is emotionally changed from the external workplace.

Bottom line: Change is inevitable. We can learn to go with the flow, laugh about what changes we like and don't like (granted that's difficult to do in the middle of middle school), learn more so we understand more, and live in gratitude that humankind *changed* from caveman grunts to complex cogitation, eventually allowing *homo sapiens* to ponder cosecants.

Keep a Perspective

"If you break your neck, if you have nothing
to eat, if your house is on fire, then you got a
problem. Everything else is inconvenience."
—Robert Fulghum[40]

It's understandable that we get upset when things don't work when we paid good money for them; or when things are not as they could be because of someone else's incompetence; or when someone doesn't follow through on a promise; or when things break down right when we need them. It's understandable that we get upset when things just don't go right.

The above quote reminds us to keep a perspective. Most of the problems and aggravations that you and I have are *inconveniences*—problems that someone in Burundi or Liberia would consider "problems of a trillionaire."

While you and I might shake our heads when someone is upset that his yacht's kitchen staff ran out of caviar in the middle of a party, that's what our problems look like to someone living in the Favelas of Brazil.

Ask someone in Sierra Leone if she would rather be upset that her car has a flat tire or at the inability to find food, any food at all.

Ask someone in South Sudan if he would rather be upset that the remote for his new flat-screen TV doesn't work or be trapped in a terrorist camp.

Ask someone in Mozambique if she would rather be angry about user-unfriendly websites or have to walk several miles to get a bucket of water.

Of course we get upset when things don't work when they should work! Problems are problems, and frustration and irritation are understandable. But <u>keep a perspective</u>. Virtually all our problems can be resolved or remedied in some way, even if the resolution is not ideal. There are persons in this world who are experiencing problems you and I can't imagine that are un-remedy-able.

Go ahead and be upset when the toaster, microwave, and computer all break down on the same day, 24 hours after the warranty expired, but keep a perspective: 60% of the world's population has no access to toilets.[41]

HELPING THE WORLD TO HEAL WITHOUT PROTESTS, POLITICS, OR MONEY

"How wonderful it is that nobody need wait a single moment before starting to improve the world."
—Anne Frank[42]

If Anne Frank, a 12-year-old girl, hiding in an attic, living in fear of being killed by Nazis, can make the world a better place, so can we!

How can we make the world a better place without protests, politics, or money?

- Smile more.

- Say thank you to others and to the divine.

- Notice what beauty is around you.

- Focus on what's right instead of what's wrong.

- Pick up one piece of litter.

- Be grateful for what you have instead of resentful of what you don't have.

- Be grateful for what you can do instead of resentful of what you can't do.

- Be polite to the rude clerk.

- Surrender past hurts by forgiving someone.

- Pray for the highest good for someone you don't like.

- Sing a happy song for no reason.

- Pray for the world, the environment, endangered species.

- Change judgment into "I'm curious" statements (e.g., I'm curious why she tattooed her whole body; I'm curious what made him so mean).

- Each morning upon waking and each evening before falling asleep, picture the Earth surrounded in healing love. Use no words. Just image the world in love and light.

Notice that **none of the above suggestions requires protests, politics, or money**. Really, friends, if Anne Frank can make the world a better place by remaining hopeful and positive in an unimaginably despairing situation, so can we!

RESPOND RATHER THAN REACT

"Before you marry a person, you should
first make them use a computer with slow
Internet to see who they really are."
—Will Ferrell[43]

Most folks are likable when they're in a good mood and life is going smoothly; it's how we react to the bumps in life that shows one's true character. When the going gets tough, those negative traits we work so hard to hide just POP OUT!

Rough spots include but are not limited to:

*Slow Internet, usually at a time when we actually *need* the computer instead of just playing on it

*Uncharitable comments made by another about us

*Traffic jams

*Discourteous/dangerous drivers

*Someone not following through on a promise

*Someone spouting different political views

*Feeling unheard

*Feeling over-tired, stressed, ill

*Major losses

*Car trouble

*Mornings for night owls

*Disappointment

*Unwanted change

*Unprofessional service

*Hearing untrue rumors about oneself

*Unmet expectations

Need I go on? Next time a bump crosses your path, notice how you react. It shows others (and yourself) your inner character. Then, once we become aware of our triggers, work on ways to **respond** rather than react.

~~~~~~

THINK BEFORE YOU SPEAK

"Is it true? Is it kind? Is it necessary? If it
doesn't meet all those requirements,
don't say it."
—Socrates[44]

Often we believe something to be true because someone we like told us it is true. Often we believe something to be true because our favorite political party told us it is true; or our family told us it is true; or the institutional church told us it is true; or the 24/7 news channels told us it is true.

Before accepting something as *true*, <u>question it</u>. Is it an actual *fact*, or is it an *opinion*? Is it verified by a neutral source, or is it hearsay? Does it explore *why* the opposite side holds the position it holds? Before accepting something as *true*, <u>question it</u>.

OK, let's say it's true. Is it **kind**? Often we say things that are unkind, even if they are true. Why would we do that? Because it makes one feel superior to cut down another.

Note well: *kind* is not the same as *nice*. It is kind to tell someone they have spinach in their teeth even though it might be considered "not nice" to mention it. However, if it saves the person from embarrassment down the road, it is kind to inform them, even if the moment of spinach-mentioning feels awkward.

Niceness avoids difficult conversations; sometimes that's helpful, sometimes it's not. Kindness addresses what needs addressing in a positive way. Kindness builds up another; niceness keeps the surface smooth but allows roils beneath the surface—which may cause more problems in the long run.

Jesus was always kind; he was not always nice. Whatever he said was for the ultimate benefit of the other—that's kind, even if it didn't feel good in the moment.

OK, let's say it's true and kind. Is it *necessary* to say it? Even if you have the facts on your side, and even if you say the facts kindly, is saying it all going to benefit the situation, or is it just going to put the other on the defensive, no matter how "right" you are? If speaking up is not going to benefit the situation, don't say it. If it's not necessary, why say it at all? Sometimes silence is not only golden, it's kinder than spewing facts that aren't going to help the situation. Bottom line: think before you speak.

THE INDESTRUCTIBLE SPIRIT

"The spirit is beyond destruction. No one can
bring an end to spirit which is everlasting."
—Bhagavad Gita[45]

The Bhagavad Gita is one of the holy scriptures of Hinduism; it's a Sanskrit poem that addresses knowledge, action, and love.

I claim no competence on the deep, spiritual meanings in the Bhagavad Gita. Who am I to take one verse of the Gita and expound on it like I know what I'm talking about!

With that disclaimer at the forefront, the above quote feels to me like it has a universal meaning from which all persons can benefit.

Whether one views the physical body as a temple in which the spirit dwells, or whether one views the physical body as a dense entrapment of the spirit—either way, something eternal lives on after physical death.

And for those who believe there is no soul, consider Einstein's statement that energy cannot be created or destroyed; it just changes forms. There is a qualitative difference between a live body and a dead body. The "aliveness" is a form of energy, and upon cessation of active functioning of the physical body, well, that aliveness-energy doesn't just stop being energy because: energy cannot be destroyed. There is some form of "afterlife," for lack of a better word. Einstein says so; Plato says so; Jesus says so; Judaism says so; Islam says so; Buddhism says so; the Bhagavad Gita says so.

(Whether the *afterlife* is understood as Sheol, Heaven, Allah, Oneness, or a Universal Energy Field is a choice of the individual; whether life is a one-time trip of the soul to earth or merely one visit on the Wheel of reincarnations is another topic for another time.)

Acknowledging that some form of energy lives on after physical death, how does this belief influence and inform our physical time on earth?

For one thing, it keeps problems in perspective. "Earthly" problems range from mildly annoying to destroying-the-body threatening. But no matter where the problem falls on the problem-continuum, there is an end to the problem, be it resolution in this lifetime or complete dissipation of the problem after "death." <u>There is temporal limitation on *all* earthly problems</u>. Keep this in mind with everything from unhelpful customer service to an unwanted medical diagnosis. "This, too, shall pass" is one of the givens in earthly life. Whether it passes because the computer modem finally connected, or whether it passes because cancer is no longer a problem on the other side of the veil remains to be seen . . . but it shall definitely pass, whatever "it" is. All earthly problems have a time-limitation on them. Realizing this helps keep a perspective.

Another way I find the above quote helpful: it reminds me I *have* a body, but I am not my body. This takes away any fear of death. "I" cannot be destroyed. In this life you may defeat me, but you cannot destroy the "me-ness" of me.

Yes, the physical body will die—be it from natural causes, accidents, murder, suicide—the physical body is at some point going to cease functioning, and at some point, even with embalming, the physical body will decay—but the spirit will not. Our spirit (alive-ness energy) is part of the eternal Universal Spirit Energy which cannot be destroyed.

We are spiritual beings on a human journey.

I make no claims to understand the sacred scriptures of Hinduism, but the above quote feels to me like it has a universal meaning from which all persons can benefit.

SEEING ALL PERSONS AS PERSONS

"You can easily judge the character of a man by how
he treats those who can do nothing for him."
—Johann Wolfgang von Goethe[46]

Years ago I was at lunch with a colleague. When the waiter came, my colleague snapped at the waiter and belittled him. It wasn't quite enough for me to challenge my colleague's behavior on the spot, but it was enough to make me embarrassed and uncomfortable. The situation was awkward, and it showed me an aspect of this person's character that heretofore was underneath the respectful surface-attitude afforded to me.

How we treat those who can do nothing for us exposes our true character. In the above vignette, I would challenge the idea that waiters "can do nothing for us." But too often, those in service positions are treated as *lesser than*.

When we shout at someone, that means we see the other as *lesser than*.

When we ignore someone, that means we see the other as *lesser than*.

When we refuse to forgive, that means we see ourselves as *greater than*.

When we judge someone, that means we see ourselves as *greater than.*

Wars and holocausts start because we see the other as lesser than and ourselves as greater than. Molehills turn into mountains because we see the other as lesser than; prejudice comes from seeing ourselves as greater than.

Conflict—global or personal—comes when we don't see the other as *a person.* The drug-induced gangbanger is still *a person.* Yes, there should be harsh consequences to violent, drug-induced behavior; no, the person shouldn't be seen as sub-human beyond redemption.

How we treat those who can do nothing for us shows our character.

~~~~~~

ANGRY GRINCH OR HAPPY HORTON?

"You have brains in your head. You have feet in your
shoes. You can steer yourself any direction you choose."
—Dr. Seuss[47]

Any direction you choose, any direction indeed, but take care, my friend, lest anger mislead.

And what about grief, hold on or let go? With God in your heart, the answer you'll know.

Forgiveness and joy are not hocus pocus; forgiveness and joy should get all our focus.

When we're ready to move a bit closer to God, smile for no reason—it's not a bit odd.

Smiling is energy that heals you and me—and him, her, and them, and the trees and the sea!

Yes, smiling will help make us make better choices, and smiling will help us to hear nature's voices.

Picture the Grinch before his heart grew; picture Horton the elephant—he's kind through and through.

Which of those images, Grinch scowl or kind smile—which of those images reflects your own style?

Perhaps it is time to let go of that frown, for Grinch frowns and sneers just bring us all down.

Smiles and deep gratitude are like peaceful white doves; they alter our spirits to embrace and share love.

LOOK ON THE LIGHT SIDE!

"Angels can fly because they take themselves lightly."
—G.K. Chesterton[48]

Of course there are serious things that take a serious attitude to address:

World hunger	Pollution	Extinction of species
Sexism	Child abuse	Arrogance
Childhood bullying	Poverty	Prejudice
Animal abuse	Abuse of any kind	Economic Inequality
Racism	Sweatshops	Crime
Supremacy	War	Ageism

Of course there are serious things that take a serious attitude to address . . .

. . . But

Whether your hair is perfectly styled is not on the list of serious things that take a serious attitude to address.

Whether your clothes are from a name-brand boutique or a rummage sale is not on the list of serious things that take a serious attitude to address.

Whether that homemade loaf of bread has more in common with a brick than with a cloud is not on the list of serious things that take a serious attitude to address.

(I solved the non-perfectly-styled-hair issue by buying three colorful bandanas as a public service act so no one has to look at my hair that I didn't bother styling.)

(I solved the brand-name v rummage sale clothes conundrum by choosing the rummage sale and laughing all the way to the bank with the money I saved.)

(I solved the homemade-bread-that-has-more-in-common-with-a-brick situation by cutting the loaf in half, giving one half to each of two friends and recommending that they toast it before trying to bite into it.)

There are some personal characteristics that should, indeed, be taken seriously, e.g., dignity; honesty in business transactions; compassion; forgiveness; promptitude; generosity; respect; decency; kindness ....

BUT: Even those desirable virtues can turn into holier-than-thou vices if one takes them *too* seriously.

Can you laugh at yourself when you make a mistake?

Do you get upset if others don't take your opinion as fact?

Can you look imperfect and not fret that you look imperfect?

Don't take yourself so seriously! Look on the light side of life even in the midst of discussing heavy issues! Angels can fly because they take themselves so lightly!

Are You a Giraffe Or a Gigantopithecus?

"It is not the strongest of the species that survive, nor the most intelligent, but the one most responsive to change."
—Charles Darwin[49]

Most of us grew up learning that Darwin coined the phrase "survival of the fittest." Not only did Darwin _not_ say that phrase, he argued against it!

Darwin said that the individual in a species who can best adapt to change is the one to survive.

Take the giraffe, for example. Millions of years ago, the giraffe was a short-necked creature. With a diet of grass and leaves, the shortest-necked giraffes had no trouble reaching grass—but it limited their food sources to grass and low-hanging leaves. The longer-necked giraffes could access not only grass and low-hanging leaves but also mid-hanging leaves. Those individual giraffes were more likely to survive because of more food sources. Over time—and "over time" means millions of years— as male longer-necked giraffes mated with female longer-necked giraffes, the species as a whole developed six-foot necks, ergo: the species survived.

And then there's the poor Gigantopithecus—the 10-foot-tall ape. A couple million years ago, Gigantopithecuses lived in harmony with humans. And then came an ice age, and the herbivore giant ape watched as its food sources disappeared due to both climate change and humans snatching up much of the edible vegetation. The Gigantopithecus didn't adapt quickly enough, and unfortunately, this non-adaptation led to extinction. If enough individual Gigantopithecuses had adapted and mated with enough other individual Gigantopithecuses that had adapted, the species as a whole might have survived.

An aside: Species extinction due to nature's natural cycles is unavoidable. Species extinction due to human corruption of the ecosystem is on us. But I digress.

For both the giraffe and Gigantopithecus, <u>adaptation</u> saved the individual, and in the giraffe's case, it saved the species. Generally speaking, people don't like to adapt, nor do institutions and businesses.

Individuals don't like to adapt to new understandings of what it means for a society to be inclusive; we haven't done well with "it takes a village to raise a child" because, well, *I* would have to sacrifice my privileges for someone else's kid.

Institutions don't like to adapt because it worked in the 1950s, didn't it!

Businesses don't like to adapt because going green and paying better wages would adversely affect profit margins.

An aside: I have no problem with individuals making a lot of money. I do have a problem with exorbitant salaries being made at the expense of the lowest-rung worker's salary. But I digress again.

One of my greatest challenges is technology. I still have trouble swiping a phone screen to answer a call. What is your personal adapting-challenge? How are you going to address this challenge: as a giraffe or a Gigantopithecus?

BLOOM WHERE YOU'RE PLANTED

"Things work out best for those who make
the best of how things work out."
—John Wooden[50]

When I was a young teenager, our church youth group went to camp . . . except I didn't want to go. I told my mom I didn't want to go, that I didn't like camping; that I couldn't sleep with five other people in a small cabin; that I didn't like outdoor activities; that I didn't want to walk in the woods where spiders might land on my head and crawl in my ear. I just didn't want to go. Mom said, "Well, you're going, and *you'll have as much fun as you allow yourself to have.*"

Hmmm. Mom was right. Again. While I didn't sleep well and didn't trust 8-legged creatures to stay away from my ears, I did my best to enjoy the experience, and voila! I had more fun than I expected. (More accurately, it wasn't as bad as I expected, but I'm choosing the more positive phrasing of "I had more fun than I expected" for the sake of remaining true to the spirit of this reflection.)

Recall the adage: *Play the hand you're dealt as best you can.* Sometimes life deals you a royal flush; sometimes you get a pair of deuces; sometimes you don't even get deuces and have to bluff. But if one folds every time one isn't dealt a royal flush, one will very rarely get to play at all.

My favorite variation of Wooden's quote is *Bloom where you're planted.* Doing your best in whatever situation you find yourself will serve your spirit better than grousing and grumping. Bloom where you're planted and play the hand you're dealt as best you can because . . . things work out best for those who make the best of how things work out.

I CHOOSE TO BE HAPPY NOW

"Now and then it's good to pause in our
pursuit of happiness and just be happy."
—Guillaume Apollinaire[51]

Many people, all through their lives, think they will be happy when they . . . (graduate) (get a job) (get a better job) (get married) (get divorced) (get a bigger house) (get a better car) (meet up with the family) (get away from the family) (get through the surgery) (have more money) (retire) . . .

As Mr. Apollinaire says, if we keep *pursuing* happiness, we'll never actually *experience* happiness.

Pursuing goals, wants, desires, betterment is normal and healthy, but when we think we won't be happy *until* . . . then we'll never be truly happy because we've pushed away *feeling* happy until some future point.

There is always something to be happy about, even in the midst of yucky days. At the very least, we can be happy that the divine PRESENCE never leaves us no matter what. Even if you don't believe in the traditional image of God as an old white man who looks suspiciously like Zeus sitting in the sky, there is a PRESENCE of goodness surrounding you. If there were not ultimate goodness, there would be no such things as kindness, grace, joy, laughter, compassion. All those good feelings have their source in the Ultimate Goodness. (A case for Plato's Ideal

Forms could be made here, but I don't know enough about it to make a credible case; might be worth checking out, though.)

Society's standard greeting is "How ya doing?" When I am asked this by sales clerks, library clerks, customer service representatives, bank tellers, strangers on the street—when I am asked "How ya doing?" I always respond "I choose to be good!"—and I add a smile to go with my response. Most times they respond with a variation of "What a wonderful way to be!"

. . . and it is a *wonderful* way to be!

While it may feel counterintuitive, tell yourself that you are happy—whether you feel happy in the moment or not. Just tell yourself you are happy. When asked by a sales clerk, etc., "How ya doing?", consider responding "I choose to be good!" or "I choose to be happy!" Unless you are in private consultation with your doctor, listing everything that's wrong isn't conducive to a productive social conversation following your litany of ills. Consider responding "I choose to be good" or "I choose to be happy." Those simple responses might just encourage the other person to inch towards feeling happy.

By repeatedly telling yourself you are happy, over time, your mind and spirit will actually believe you *are* happy, in the moment; and the mind and spirit will learn that "happiness is an inside job." Who knows, maybe tomorrow you might be happy without even trying!

PEACE IS HEALING AND HEALING IS PEACE

"Life will give you whatever experience is most helpful
for the evolution of your consciousness. How do you
know this is the experience you need? Because this
is the experience you are having at the moment."
—Eckhart Tolle[52]

The purpose of religion is to bring us into deeper relationship with the PRESENCE. Sacraments, rituals, parables, dogma, beliefs, etc., are *tools* to help us connect more deeply with the PRESENCE.

Another *tool* that can help us connect more deeply with the Divine is *experiences.*

Every situation, event, chapter in life that we *experience* is an opportunity to respond in ways that connect us more deeply with The Great Spirit.

If we believe the Divine to be pure Goodness, and if we believe this Goodness is present everywhere at all times, and if we believe nothing can separate us from this Goodness, then this means the divine Goodness is present in *all* experiences.

So how do we reconcile what feels bad with this idea of "All-Present-Goodness"?

My personal belief is *not* that God ordains "bad" things to test or punish us. Human ignorance, arrogance, greed, fear, etc., cause humans to act in ways that do *not* bring a deeper connection into the PRESENCE, and those "bad" experiences are consequences of human choices. Sometimes those icky-consequence experiences come from our own actions, and sometimes we are unfortunate bystanders of others' actions.

But because the divine Goodness from which we cannot be separated is ever-present, those experiences we deem "bad" are opportunities to transcend negative reactions. By rising above the hurt, we break the chain of negativity and move into deeper relationship with the Sacred Spirit. When that happens, there is no greater "good" that a human can experience!

Extreme situations, such as the Holocaust, are the result of indescribably, unconscionably poor actions. But even in that despicable experience, the victims had the choice to embrace despair or embrace trust that the PRESENCE was with them, even unto death. Clinging to the PRESENCE in the midst of horror would give one's soul *peace* . . . peace in the midst of calamity and terror.

In other words, whatever situation enters our path, it is an opportunity to learn what responses lead away from and what responses lead toward a deeper relationship with the divine Goodness—which is experienced as peace.

While a descriptive phrase might be "every situation is an opportunity to learn a lesson," the phrase *learn a lesson* has connotations of punitiveness . . . and yet, there is nothing punitive about deepening our relationship with God.

For example, if I need to learn patience, life will present me with opportunities to develop patience; if I need to learn forgiveness, life will present me with opportunities to forgive. As Eckhart Tolle says: *Life will give you whatever experience is most helpful for the evolution of your consciousness.*

Some physical and mental illnesses are "consequences" of the frailty of the human body; we can use these illnesses as opportunities to rise above fear and despair and as catalysts to transform society into a place where all those in the throes of dis-ease are cared for.

When we connect with The Spirit of God, we are at peace. When we are at peace, we are healed. Healing is feeling at peace whether dis-ease is present or not, simply because *God* is present.

Tenderness Is Not Doormatness. The Pope Says So.

"Tenderness is the path of choice for the strongest,
most courageous men and women."
—Pope Francis[53]

Tenderness takes the time to understand where the other is coming from.

Tenderness looks with compassion at fear disguised as meanness.

Tenderness listens to learn, not just waits its turn to speak.

Tenderness knows forgiveness heals the *forgiver's* soul.

You've heard the expression, "When the going gets tough, the tough get going." By extension, when the tough get going, the going gets even tougher for those of us who weren't all that tough in the first place. And all we're going to end up with is a really tough world.

It takes strength to be tender.

CONTENT IS NOT THE SAME
AS PASSIVE RESIGNATION

"If you look at what you have in life, you'll
always have more. If you look at what you don't
have in life, you'll never have enough."
—Oprah Winfrey[54]

"Go-getters" might argue one should never be content and satisfied with what one has because there is always more to be had, a higher rung on the ladder to climb, a better future if one has the chutzpah to go get it.

Here's what the "go-getters" don't understand: *content* and *satisfied* mean being at peace and grateful for what one has, for where one is in the moment. They do *not* mean *resignation*; they do *not* mean "don't work anymore to improve oneself."

Feeling content and satisfied allows one to not only live in gratitude, it also allows for a more focused approach to what one *needs* for "betterment."

Without contentment, satisfaction, and gratitude, one loses perspective on how much money is enough; how many rungs on the corporate ladder really need to be climbed. Without contentment, satisfaction, and gratitude, there's no time to smell the roses; no time to let the body-mind-spirit heal with a stroll in nature; often relationships are sacrificed for that next rung, simply because there is no contentment.

Some folks approach a situation from the negative: "I do not have enough money." However, approaching the situation from this discontented angle may mean that the person will never feel he has enough money because there is no solid definition of what "financial security" means.

Consider approaching the situation from the positive: "I am content with what I have now. I am grateful to have as much as I have. I shall work to procure X number of dollars by the end of the year so I can pay off the Visa bill." This mindset allows one to feel grateful and at peace (satisfied and contented) while working for "more" (whatever "more" means), and it allows for the healthy perspective that even though I don't have ____ in the moment, I'm still OK.

As Irv Blitzer said in *Cool Runnings,* "A gold medal is a wonderful thing. But if you're not enough without it, you'll never be enough with it."

BE OPEN TO LEARNING

"The difference between stupidity and
genius is that genius has its limits."
—Albert Einstein[55]

To get started, let's note the difference between *dumb* and *stupid*. While "dumb" and "stupid" have multiple meanings, for the purpose of this reflection, "dumb" shall indicate a person who lacks intellectual skills; "stupid" shall indicate a person who has the intellect to act rationally and appropriately—but doesn't.

It's not that "dumb" people can't learn; it just takes longer, and there probably is a cap to the number of abstract concepts one can comprehend...but "dumb" people *can* learn.

Stupidity, as stated above, means one has the capability for rational functioning, but, for whatever reason, opts for the irrational choice. While, as the maxim goes, "Ya can't fix stupid," there is a chance that the person can gain maturity after enough stupid acts spawn enough negative consequences.

The mindset I have the most trouble dealing with is *closed-mindedness*. Closed-mindedness *refuses* to learn; closed-mindedness *chooses* ignorance over knowledge. I don't get it. I just don't get closed-mindedness.

Probably most people would not describe themselves as closed-minded, but...

- Is your image of God the same as what your third-grade Sunday School teacher told you, and—by God!—you're not going to change your image of God?!?

- Do you renounce all concepts of God because you don't like the way Bible-thumpers have hijacked the image of God and therefore any and all concepts of God are unpalatable?

- Do you disbelieve everything the *other* political party says and believe whatever your political party says?

- Do you dismiss Eastern techniques for healing and wellness because your Western-oriented doctor dismisses them?

- Do you dismiss Western medical procedures because your Eastern-oriented healthcare provider doesn't trust Western medicine?

- Do you believe *all* metaphysical concepts are woo-woo?

- Prejudice, bigotry, and hatred are taught; no baby is born hating something. As children, we cannot control what we are taught; as adults, however, we need to take responsibility to reevaluate those negative lessons. Have you reevaluated what you were taught about "those people"?

- When you hear of an event, do you automatically look for truth on both sides of the story, or do you have your mind made up before hearing what each side says? Consider the following vignette:

A group of people takes food and money downtown and distributes it to the homeless and drug-users.

—Is this a group of do-gooders who has no long-term understanding of how to fix a long-term problem and is wasting money on people who won't be helped for more than a day?

OR

—Is this a group of people who sees a need and believes the money is well-spent, providing at least temporary assistance for those who no longer can take care of themselves?

Closed-mindedness chooses one of the above stances without considering the merits of the other stance—and <u>both stances have valid points</u>!!

At best, closed-mindedness prevents one from developing mentally, emotionally, and spiritually. At worst, it's catastrophic, e.g., denial of climate change. Scientists are jumping up and down, waving red flags, shouting that every ecosystem is in critical danger, and species are going extinct because their habitats are beyond repair. If closed-mindedness continues to deny this inconvenient truth, then we've got *deadly* consequences.

I don't get it; I just don't get closed-mindedness.

I guess I'm closed-minded about closed-mindedness. Hmmm. I'll have to think about that.

OPINION V FACT: DON'T CONFUSE THE TWO!

> "The difference between a pizza and your
> opinion is that I only asked for the pizza."
> —Anonymous[56]

Opinions are not bad. They do, however, become troublesome when they are presented as fact, or as the only "right" opinion.

The word *opinion* comes from the Latin word *opinio* meaning "to think or believe." "To think or believe" is not the same as "fact." By definition, an opinion leaves room for different thinking and believing. While we may diametrically disagree with another's opinion, while we may deem another opinion as uninformed, while we may perceive another opinion as selfish—for better or worse, *opinions* allow room for differences.

Conflict comes when we attempt to present our opinion as fact, or as the only "right" thinking. Of course we believe our opinion is "right," or we wouldn't hold that opinion in the first place! But militantly shoving our opinion at another person does not invite the other to consider the merits of our beliefs. What it does is put the other person on the defensive, and if the other person is on the defensive, he's not in a place where he's willing to hear *why* we hold the opinion we do.

When presented with an opinion with which you disagree, perhaps responding with "I'm curious why you think that" or "Help me understand why you believe that" will avoid contention or help diffuse any contention already present . . . but it will avoid or diffuse contention only if we <u>listen to understand</u>.

In a conversation you may learn what the other has experienced that persuades her to embrace that opinion. Listening to understand may give insight you hadn't thought of, and an insight you hadn't thought of does NOT mean you need to change *your* opinion. It does, however, help you understand where the other is coming from.

If asked for your opinion, by all means give it, but consider giving it in a tone that acknowledges it's an *opinion*. And if you are not asked for your opinion, it shows maturity to refrain from giving your opinion.

Be mindful that non-verbal responses are sometimes more powerful than words: rolling one's eyes; shaking one's head; looking away; snorting; a dismissive sigh; a glare—those are non-verbal ways of giving your opinion of another's opinion, and they are not helpful.

Letting the other know she is heard, exploring why he holds that opinion, and presenting one's own opinion as an *opinion* makes sharing a pizza more enjoyable.

IF YOU NEED HELP,
FOR PETE'S SAKE, ASK FOR HELP

"I walk around like everything is fine, but deep
down, inside my shoe, my sock is sliding off."
—Anonymous[57]

So . . . your sock is sliding off inside your shoe. What should you do? If you're able, bend down and pull it back up. Bunched-up sock is not comfortable. And unless asked directly, no one wants to hear about it. Just pull up your sock and be on your way.

But what if you are not able to bend down and pull up your sock? For Pete's sake, ask for help! Too often we don't ask for help out of **_pride_**. Pride is considered the deadly sin from which all other sins are spawned. (Yes, there is a "good" kind of pride, as in taking pride in one's work, a feeling of dignity. We're not talking about that vibration of pride. There's also a pride of lions. We're not talking about that, either.)

The negative vibrations of pride include an exaggerated sense of one's own self-worth . . . as in "people will think less of me if I ask for help."

I've come up with some reasons why some folks don't ask for help when needed:

1. We don't want to be a bother to others.

2. We've seen other people ask for help when they don't really need it, and we don't want to be like them.

3. We used to be able to bend down and pull up our own sock, but age or illness or frailty has limited what we are now capable of doing, and we don't want to admit to ourselves that we can't pull up our own socks anymore, so we live with the uncomfortableness.

4. We don't want others to know we need help.

I get that we don't want to be a bother to others; I get that we don't want to be like those who feel entitled to help when they don't need it. But both of those reasons have pride in them, just as reasons 3 and 4 do.

Up until some years ago, I would spend a very long day— 12+hours—deep-cleaning my house: everything off every shelf so every item and every shelf could be cleaned; every piece of furniture moved so the furniture and underneath the furniture could be cleaned; everything washable was washed . . .

and then one year, it took two days of 8+ hours to get the same amount of work done . . .

and then the next year I decided that the underbelly of the couch didn't really need cleaning because no one has ever entered my house, tipped over the couch, and checked to see how much dust was on the bottom of the couch...

then the next year, "deep-cleaning" was modified to "semi-deep cleaning" . . .

and now, a "good wipe-over" constitutes "cleaning the house."

There may come a time when I can't do even a "good wipe-over." OK, then I'll ask for help.

Just because we can't do what we used to do doesn't mean we are now unworthy, wretched creatures without value. What it means is that we can't do what we used to do. Period. And if we refuse to acknowledge we can't do what we used to do, and if we refuse to ask for help when needed, then that's **_pride_**. Ask any spiritual teacher if that's a good thing. (Hint: the answer is _no_. That kind of pride is _not_ a good thing.)

Asking for help when needed is especially important—extremely important—when the issue is mental and emotional health. Talking with a mental health professional does not indicate weakness. Take this to heart, friend. There is NO disgrace in seeking professional help. Get the kind of help you need if you need help.

Bonus tip: receive the help _graciously_. Graciousness shows appreciation that someone cares enough to help.

It shows wisdom to ask for help when needed.

It shows gratitude to accept help graciously.

It shows unhealthy pride not to ask for help when needed.

MORNING MEDITATION WORTHY OF TAPING ON YOUR REFRIGERATOR

"Every day, think as you wake up:
Today I am fortunate to have woken up.
I am alive, I have a precious human life.
I am not going to waste it.
I am going to use all my energies to develop myself,
to expand my heart out to others,
to achieve enlightenment for the benefit of all beings.
I am going to have kind thoughts towards others.
I am not going to get angry or think badly about others.
I am going to benefit others as much as I can."
—His Holiness The XIV Dalai Lama[58]

The Dalai Lama knows we're not going to get the above sentiment perfect every day. So! It's not about being perfect; it's about healing and deepening life's journey, one day at a time.

Consider taping this thought on your refrigerator so you see it every day.

What Does It Mean to "Act Your Age"?

"I don't know how to act my age because
I've never been this old before."
—Anonymous[59]

When someone says, "Act your age!" she usually means, "Don't embarrass yourself," or "Don't embarrass me when I'm with you."

Not acting in an embarrassing manner generally means *follow the conventional rules of society.* That can either be good advice . . . or stifling.

As an upper-middle-aged woman, I don't dress so that my undergarments show; ain't nobody's business what my bra straps look like. In that regard, I dress like a woman of my age "should." However, I don't give a hoot that my purple shirt with maroon sweatpants and green socks don't match (a color combination appealing to three-year-olds). Don't care that they don't match, and don't care if you do care.

If I wanted a '64 Mustang 289 V8, who's to say that's not a car a woman my age should be driving! (For the record, I do not want a '64 Mustang 289 V8; but if I did, why shouldn't I?)

Admittedly, there are contexts that inform age-appropriate behavior. For example, when my grandson was two years old, I was 57 years old. He and I went to the park by my house that has a playground with a slide. The first time we went, he didn't want to go down the slide, so I went down the slide first. He went after me and loved it. But he wouldn't go down the slide again unless I went first again. So that day, I went down the slide a dozen times, and so did he as long as he could follow me.

Anybody watching us might have thought how cute it is that Grammy is going down the slide with her adorable grandson!

But it was only cute because my adorable grandson was with me. If I had gone to the playground by myself—without a child—and gone down the slide a dozen times

. . . well, that's weird at best, creepy at worst.

So up front I admit that there are contexts in which age-appropriate behavior should be informed by societal norms.

But perhaps, just perhaps, we too often let conventional norms stifle us.

If you're 60 years old and want to go skinny dipping in the south of France where it's legal to do so, then go do it, and don't let anyone tell you to "act your age"!

If you're 70 years old and want to take up disco dancing, then go do it, and don't let anyone tell you to "act your age"!

If you're 80 years old and want to dye your hair pink and cut it in a punk-rock style, then go do it, and don't let anyone tell you to "act your age"!

At any age, if you want to wear a purple shirt with maroon sweat-pants and green socks, then do it, and don't let anyone tell you to "act your age"!

If you're over 20 years old and want to go to a child's playground by yourself and slide down a structure built for a 2-year-old, ***don't*** do it. That's just creepy.

WHERE???

"I never really wanted to go to Japan. Simply because I don't like eating fish. And I know that's very popular out there in Africa."
—Britney Spears[60]

Where to start!

Well, let's start with the obvious:

1.   Japan is not in Africa.

2.   There is more to do in Japan than eat fish.

The quote itself is funny! The ignorance behind it is not.

From where does this level of ignorance originate?

Consider this: Generally speaking, our schools focus on training students to do well on standardized tests so the school district can get more funding. The problem is not what the tests emphasize; the problem, as I see it, is what is sacrificed to train students for these tests, namely: social studies; world history; arts and music; anthropology; geography; multi-cultural awareness.

Of course students need to be taught math and science! But when social studies, etc., is deemed unimportant, we end up with graduates who don't know where Japan is.

When enough adults don't know "where Japan is," we develop into a society that perceives any culture different than our own as "other" instead of "another." On one level, I'm playing with semantics here; on a deeper level, I'm naming a systemic ill. When "different" is perceived as "otherness," and "otherness" is perceived as "wrong," prejudice is born.

If we are not taught as children the value of different cultures, different types of music, different art forms; if we are not taught as children that a religion other than our own is simply a different way of worshiping THE SACRED SOURCE (insert whatever name for God you want), then supremacy rears its ugly head.

One person not knowing "where Japan is" is sad; a society not appreciating the value of different cultures, religions, art, music, native dress, etc., is dangerous.

The devaluation of "anotherness" deserves more attention than this reflection can offer. So let's end with some upbeat fun that engages our focus beyond our borders.

What follows is a just-for-fun quiz. See how many entries in the left-hand column you can match up with its country in the right-hand column. Some are obvious, some can be figured out, and maybe some will be challenging. Consider learning more about any incorrect answers—just for fun.

(Answers are found at the end of the book.)

Shche ne vmerla	France
Mesopotamia	Scotland
Sgian-dubh	Iran
Omdurman	Antarctica
Black Forest	China
Hanfu	Sudan
Kilimanjaro	Iraq
Ein Sof	Ukraine
-128.6 F, Vostok	Germany
Zoroastrianism	Tanzania
Echidna	Israel
Lascaux Grotto	Australia

How many did you get correct? Great!

How many did you get incorrect? Great!—because incorrect answers are an invitation to learn about something; enjoy the journey of expanding your knowledge of "another-ness."

~~~~~~

EPILOGUE

So . . .

For which of the reflections did you think, "Yes! She was right on with this one!"?

For which of the reflections did you think, "Don't know about this; will have to think more about it"?

For which of the reflections did you think, "Nope. Not going there"?

For which of the reflections did you think, "After reading this, I've changed my mind because I never thought about it that way before"?

. . . *Why?*

Why did you resonate (or not) with a particular reflection? In other words; what deeper value did the reflection touch that either affirmed or challenged your thinking?

If even one of the reflections inspired you to think about something in a different way; if even one of the reflections evoked a desire to learn more about something; if even one of the reflections spurred conversation, then this book served its purpose, and it is my privilege to have shared this part of your journey with you. May you continue to go deep and think about your thoughts as you step forward in life. May you reflect and find your own thoughtful path forward.

Namaste.

ABOUT THE AUTHOR

Audrey Alexander, a St. Louis native, has a Bachelor of Science degree in Psychology, Sociology, and Philosophy, and is trained in Quantum Touch healing. Audrey enjoys moments at the Missouri Botanical Gardens. Since five years old, Audrey has enjoyed her rescue dogs.

"Some of my greatest joys in life are from making people laugh and inspiring people to learn. It's a blessing when both happen at the same time! ☺"

ENDNOTES

1   google.com/search?q=cicero+gratitude+is+not+only

2   coolfunnyquotes.com/author/anonymous/slam-revolving-door

3   Thich Nhat Hahn. *Peace Is Every Step.* Bantam Books: New York. 1991. p. 38.

4   goodreads.com/author/quotes/11784.David_R_Hawkins

5   quote from John 8:7b CEV; cf John 8:2-11 for the context of the quote.

6   https://quotes.thefamouspeople.com/chief-seattle-1043.php

7   For a comprehensive exegesis of Genesis 1, confer: The New Interpreter's Bible Volume 1. Abingdon Press: Nashville. 1994. Leander E. Keck, Sr. Ed. *The Book of Genesis: Introduction, Commentary, and Reflections.* Terence E. Fretheim.

8   goodreads.com/quotes/532981-never-follow-anyone-else's-path

9   google.com/search?q=quote+rajesh+Khanna+with+time+we+have+become+increasingly+familiar

10   brainyquote.com/quthors/carl-jung-quotes-there-is-no-such-thing-as-a-pure-introvert

11   quotefancy.com/quote/1278974/Jack-Kornfield-What-would-we-have-to-hold-in-compassion-to-be-at-peace-right-now

[12] brainyquote.com/quotes/abraham_lincoln_105870

[13] google.com/search?q=mother+teresa+i+will+never+attend

[14] google.com/search?q=who+said+if+the+only+prayer

[15] www.google.com/search?gs_ssp=eJzj4tLP1TfIS8sxqEw2YPSS
TMzLS1XISczNLyIRKMkoSk1VKChKrEwtKgYA_oENoQ&q=
anne+lamott+three+prayers&rlz=1C1NHXL_enUS701US701&oq
=anne+l&aqs=chrome.1.69i59j46i39j46i67i433j69i57j0i67j46i2
0i131i263i433i512j69i60j69i61.12546j0j7&sourceid=chrome&
ie=UTF-8

[16] google.com/search?q=toni+morrison+definitions+belong+to+
the+definers

[17] pinterest.com/pin/69594756720854723/#

[18] inspiringquotes.us/author/1252-Muhammad/about-prophet#

[19] google.com/search?q=schrodinger+a+careful+analysis+of+the
+process

[20] goodreads.com/quotes/51841-for-small-creatures-such-as-we

[21] google.com/search?q=Seneca+quote+luck+never+made+a+
man+wise

[22] google.com/search?q=quote+Obama+the+real+test+is+not+
whether+you+avoid+failure

[23] google.com/search?q=quote+Confucius+our+our+greatest
+glory

[24] google.com/search?q=quote+edison+i+have+not+failed

[25] brainyquote.com/quotes/plato_398192

[26] brainyquote.com/quotes/booker_t_washington_122789

[27] google.com/search?q=buddha+quote+let+us+rise+up

[28] readbeach.com/quote/next-time-a-stranger-talks-to-you

[29] www.mayoclinic.org/healthy-lifestyle/stress-management/in-depth/stress-relief/art-20044456

[30] goodreads.com/quotes/551027-yesterday-I-was-clever

[31] brainyquote.com/quotes/Russell_simmons_602682#

[32] brainyquote.com/quotes/Solomon_short_388005#

[33] google.com/search?q=be+kinder+than+necessary

[34] google.com/search?q=the+trouble+with+most+of+us

[35] goodreads.com/quotes/51817-it-may-be-hard-for-an-egg-to-turn-into-a-bird

[36] parade.com/252644/viannguyen/15-of-martin-luther-king-jr-s-most-inspiring-motivationa

[37] beherenownetwork.com/Kabir-breath-inside-breath-role-guru

[38] google.com/search?q=jane+goodall+what+you+do+makes+a+difference

[39] google.com/search?q=change+is+inevitable+except+from+a+vending+machine

[40] google.com/search?q=Robert+Fulghum+quote+if+you+break

41 www.google.com/search?q=what+percentage+of+the+world+has+no+toilets&rlz=1C1NHXL_enUS701US701&oq=what+percentage+of+the+world+has+no+toilets&aqs=chrome..69i57j33i160j33i22i29i30.11422j0j7&sourceid=chrome&ie=UTF-8

42 google.com/search?=anne+frank+how+wonderful+it+is

43 quotefancy.com/quote/1185049/Will-Ferrell-Before-you-marry

44 google.com/search?q=Socrates+is+it+true+is+it+kind

45 google.com/search?q=quote+the+spirit+is+beyond+destruction+bhagavad+gita&rlz=1C1NHXL_e

46 goodreads.com/quotes/130632-you-can-easily

47 google.com/search?q=suess+you+have+brains+in+your+head

48 goodreads.com/quotes/8254513-angels-can-fly-because-they-can-take

49 quoteinvestigator.com/2014/05/04/adapt

50 goodreads.com/quotes/183589-things-work-out-best

51 krishnapendyala.com/now-and-then-it's-good to-pause

52 goodreads.com/quotes/28276-life-will-give-you (From *A New Earth*, Tolle)

53 google.com/search?q=pope+francis+tenderness+is+the+path+of+choice

54 booksameya.in/if-you-look-at-what-you-have-in-life

55 google.com/search?q=Einstein+quote+the+difference+between

[56] coolfunnyquotes.com/author/anonymous/pizza-vs-opinion/

[57] coolfunnyquotes.com/author/anonymous/walk-around-like
-everything-is-fine

[58] goodreads.com/quotes/29007-every-day-think-as-you-wake-up

[59] coolfunnyquotes.com/author/anonymous/don't-know-how-to
-act-age

[60] www.goodreads.com/quotes/148882-i-ve-never-really-want-
ed-to-go-to-japan-simply-because#

Answers to the "Where" Pop Quiz

Shche ne vmerla	Ukraine (Those are the first words to the Ukrainian national anthem)
Mesopotamia	Iraq (Mesopotamia is the area between the Tigris and Euphrates Rivers)
Sgian-dubh	Scotland (Sgian-dubh is a small knife that is part of the Scottish kilt ensemble)
Omdurman	Sudan (Omdurman is the most populated city in Sudan)
Black Forest	Germany (The Black Forest is a mountain range in Germany so named because of the copious amount of dark evergreen trees)
Hanfu	China (Hanfu is traditional Chinese clothing)
Kilimanjaro	Tanzania (Mount Kilimanjaro is the tallest mountain on the African continent and the highest free-standing mountain in the world. You can climb it if you want to. I don't want to.)

Ein Sof	Israel (Ein Sof is a sacred name for God in Jewish mysticism—Kabbalah. Ein Sof loosely translates as "The Endless One.")
-128.6 F, Vostok	Antarctica (This is the lowest temperature, Fahrenheit, recorded in Antarctica at Vostok, a Russian scientific research station.)
Zoroastrianism	Iran (Zoroastrianism is one of the oldest religions, founded by a man named Zoroaster in Iran. It teaches that there is an ongoing battle between good and evil, and that in the end, good will win. It teaches that there is one and only one God.)
Echidna	Australia (Echidnas are animals found only in Australia and look like a cross between a porcupine and an anteater. Echidnas and platypuses are the only mammals that lay eggs. Do not try to pet an echidna. They don't like that.)
Lascaux Grotto	France (Lascaux Grotto has cave paintings about 16,000 years old— give or take 10,000 years.)

Anything pique your interest to learn more?

www.ingramcontent.com/pod-product-compliance
Lightning Source LLC
Chambersburg PA
CBHW060526130626
46553CB00002B/664